BIBLE ADVE
Old Testament Heroes, Acts and Revelation

Written by Carol Ann Morrow

Illustrated by Ave O. Macasiray

ISBN 1-936020-15-7

God created man and woman and asked them to name the animals and plants in the garden of Eden. Can you name some animals and plants in their garden?

2

God told Noah to build an ark and to bring two of each animal onto it to save them from a big flood that covered the earth. Can you find any animals from Adam and Eve's garden that are on Noah's boat?

Joseph was the youngest son of his father Israel. His father gave hir
a beautiful coat, which made his brothers very jealous. It was the
beginning of many adventures for Joseph. Make his coat beautiful.

God spoke to Moses from a bush which was on fire but did not burn up. He ordered Moses to lead His people out of Egypt, where they were suffering.

Moses stretched out his hand and the sea parted so that God's people could escape from Pharaoh and his army. When the people had crossed, they thanked God for rescuing them.

6

Joshua, the next leader after Moses, led the Jewish people across the Jordan River to the walled city of Jericho. When they marched around the city blowing their horns, the walls of Jericho fell down.

Samson, a Judge of Israel who had been blinded by the Philistines, regained the strength he had from God when his hair grew back. He shook the columns of their temple until it fell down on them—and him.

Naomi, whose husband and sons had died, was sad and lonely. Her daughter-in-law, Ruth, stayed with Naomi, which was a sacrifice. In turn, Naomi introduced Ruth to Boaz, who married Ruth. They are ancestors of Jesus.

God called to young Samuel in his sleep, but Samuel thought it was someone else. After the third call, he answered, "Speak, Lord, for Your servant is listening."

The young shepherd David used a slingshot to strike down the Philistine Goliath, a very tall and experienced soldier. David, who became the leader of Israel, was the great-grandson of Ruth.

King Solomon, David's son, was a wise king of Israel who built a beautiful Temple for the Lord.

The Queen of Sheba came to visit Solomon, bringing gold and
jewels as gifts. Seeing how wise he was, she stayed to learn from
him as much as she could. Solomon gave all her gifts to the Temple.

Elijah the prophet asked a poor widow for some bread and water. She generously gave him her very last bit of food and drink. He blessed her with a supply of oil and flour that never ran out.

Elijah the prophet was taken up to heaven in a fiery chariot with flaming horses. Elisha, who had asked for a double blessing of Elijah's spirit, picked up his mantle from the ground and wore it from that time onward.

Sarah had seven husbands who all died on their wedding night. God blessed Sarah in her marriage to Tobiah. The Angel Raphael helped Tobiah very much. He told the couple to begin their marriage with prayer.

Judith was a widow of Israel. Enemies led by General Holofernes surrounded her city. Judith charmed her way into the General's tent. He drank so much that she was able to cut off his head, saving her people.

The beautiful Queen Esther pleaded for the life of the Jewish people, whom the wicked Haman had plotted to kill. She saved them all from death at the hands of the king.

Job was tested by God and suffered from hunger, loss, and sores all over his body. He did not lose faith. God showed Job all His wonders and restored him to health and happiness.

Isaiah, one of the greatest prophets, constantly reminded God's people that all good things were a gift from their Creator. An angel blessed Isaiah's lips with a glowing coal to prepare him to speak for God.

Jeremiah was also a prophet. God told him that he was to be like clay in His hands, letting God make of him whatever He wanted.

The prophet Ezekiel had a vision of a large field piled with bones. God told Ezekiel that He would bring life and hope to His people just as He could raise up these dry bones.

Daniel's three trusted helpers—Shadrach, Meshach and Abednego—were thrown into a furnace because they did not worship false gods. An angel joined them in the furnace and they were not burned.

Daniel got into trouble for praying to the One True God instead of to King Darius. Daniel was thrown to the lions, but they did not hurt him at all. This caused the King to praise the God of Daniel.

Jonah did not enjoy being a prophet. He was thrown overboard into the sea and was swallowed up by a whale. The whale spit Jonah out just in time for him to tell the people of Ninevah to turn back to God.

Zechariah the prophet had many visions of the Lord coming to save His people. He prophesied the coming of the Messiah in words that remind us of Jesus on Palm Sunday. He told Jerusalem to shout for joy, which they did on Palm Sunday.

With the power of God, the apostle Peter cured a crippled man. Peter told the people that God could do even greater things than that.

A man named Saul was knocked to the ground by lightning, which blinded him. He heard the voice of Jesus, asking him, "Saul, Saul, why are you persecuting Me?" Saul became Paul, a powerful teacher and apostle of the early Church.

Paul and his companion Silas were whipped, imprisoned, and chained for their good works done in the name of Jesus. An earthquake shook the prison, causing the door to open and let them out. This led their jailer to believe in Jesus.

The Bible's last book is the Book of Revelation, which tells us much about the end of time. A crowd too big to count stands before the throne of God, all dressed in white (like baptismal garments).

In heaven, Saint Michael the Archangel battled against the powers of evil and cast them out.

At the end of the Book of Revelation is a description of a new heavens and a new earth, where God is with us and everyone is happy. The last prayer in the Bible is "Come, Lord Jesus." We say "Amen!"